The Rourke Guide
to State Symbols

FLOWERS

Jason Cooper

The Rourke Press, Inc.
Vero Beach, Florida 32964

PHOTO CREDITS:
p. 5, 7, 12 (GA) © James Robinson; p. 10, 16 (IN), 21, 22 (MA), 26 (MO), 37 © Jerry Hennen; p. 12 (DE), 26 (MT), 31 © Tom Ulrich; p. 29 © Joe Antos; p. 35 © Wayne Elisens; p. 38 © Susan Glascock; p. 40 © Steve Bentsen; cover, p. 6, 8, 9, 11, 13, 16 (IL), 17, 18, 19, 20, 22 (MD), 23, 24, 25, 27, 28, 30, 32 (both), 33, 34, 36 (PA), 39 (both), 41, 42, 43, 44, 45, 46 (both), 47 © Lynn M. Stone; p. 14 courtesy Hawaii Visitors Bureau and Lyon Arboretum; p. 15 courtesy Idaho Department of Commerce; p. 36 (OR) courtesy Oregon Tourism Commission

ARTWORK:
Cover artwork by Jim Spence

EDITORIAL SERVICES:
Penworthy Learning Systems

Library of Congress Cataloging-in-Publication Data

Cooper, Jason, 1942 -
    Flowers / Jason Cooper.
        p. cm. — (The Rourke guide to state symbols)
    Includes index.
    Summary: Presents a description of and background information about the flowering plants that have been chosen to represent the fifty states and the District of Columbia.
    ISBN 1-57103-194-4
    1. State flowers—United States—Juvenile literature. [1. State flowers.
2. Flowers. 3. Emblems, State.]
I. Title II. Series: Cooper, Jason, 1942 -   The Rourke guide to state symbols.
QK85.C66 1997
582.13'0973—dc21   97–15367
                                                    CIP
                                                    AC

Printed in the USA

TABLE OF CONTENTS

INTRODUCTION

Flowers are loved for their beauty and sweet smell. The flowers we raise, called domestic flowers, brighten gardens, pathways, and homes. Wildflowers nod in our forests, deserts, grasslands, pastures, and sand dunes.

Flowers are used for bouquets, corsages, and displays. They are the subjects of countless paintings and photographs. Not surprisingly, each of the 50 states and the District of Columbia chose a flower to represent them. Some states repeated the choice of others so that only 44 different kinds of plants are official state flowers.

Flowers are simply blossoms. Like 22 of the state flowers, they grow on vines, trees, shrubs, and bushes as well as on typical flower plants. Oklahoma, before it became a state, chose mistletoe, a parasite. The white pine cone and tassel were the choice of Maine.

Violets (four states) and roses (four states and the District of Columbia) were popular picks. Other flowers adopted by more than one state were apple, dogwood, goldenrod, magnolia, mountain laurel, and rhododendron.

Some states chose dazzling beauties (lady's slipper in Minnesota, Rocky Mountain columbine in Colorado for example). Others picked less showy flowers (forget-me-not in Alaska, mayflower in Massachusetts). Several choices were made because the flower was found only in that state. A few state flowers, such as Florida's orange blossom, were important to that state's history or economy.

Whatever the reason for adopting it, each flower seems "right" for the state that chose it.

ALABAMA
CAMELLIA

Scientific Name: *Camellia japonica*
Year Made State Flower: 1959

The camellia is a dark green shrub that produces large showy flowers in early spring. Camellias are commonly used in gardens and groves throughout Alabama and the Southeast.

The camellia is not native to the United States. It is native to the warm parts of Asia. Like many of the state flowers, it was imported to the United States because of its beauty.

ALASKA
FORGET-ME-NOT

Scientific Name: *Myosotis alpestris*
Year Made State Flower: 1917

Alaskans chose the forget-me-not as their territorial flower long before Alaska became a state, in 1959. The blue of the little forget-me-not helps remind Alaskans of the big blue skies of their state. The gold center of the flower helps remind them of the state's gold mining history.

Forget-me-nots are common wildflowers in the 49th state. They bloom on stems 4 to 12 inches (10 - 31 centimeters) high from late June into early August.

ARIZONA
SAGUARO (GIANT CACTUS)

Scientific Name: *Cereus giganteus*
Year Made State Flower: 1901

Arizona's great, treelike cactus are eye-popping plants. The saguaro stands up to 50 feet (15 meters) tall and may have up to twenty armlike limbs. In the United States the saguaro is found only in southern Arizona. Saguaro National Park, near Tucson, preserves "forests" of these giant cacti.

Saguaros grow from desert lowlands to mountain slopes 3,600 feet (1097 meters) high.

The saguaro's white flowers grow in clusters at the tips of the huge "arms." Most of the flowering is in June. The saguaro blooms at night, but usually lasts well into the daylight hours.

ARKANSAS
APPLE BLOSSOM

Scientific Name: *Malus domestica*
Year Made State Flower: 1901

Each spring the apple trees bloom with thousands of white roselike flowers. They make an impressive sight in the orchards of Arkansas and elsewhere. Michigan (p. 23) also adopted the apple blossom as its state flower.

Stand near a blooming apple tree: It sounds like it is buzzing. The tree is not buzzing, of course, but the thousands of honeybees in the blossoms certainly are. The bees transfer grains of pollen from one blossom to another and help ensure that the blossoms will produce apples.

CALIFORNIA

GOLDEN POPPY (CALIFORNIA POPPY)

Scientific Name: *Eschscholzia californica*
Year Made State Flower: 1903

A spread of California poppies seen at a distance turn grassy hillsides into gold carpets. They are one of nature's most spectacular springtime shows in California.

Some years are much better than others for the poppy bloom. The timing and amount of rainfall are important to the growth of poppy seeds into flowers.

COLORADO
ROCKY MOUNTAIN COLUMBINE
(BLUE COLUMBINE)

Scientific Name: *Aguilegia caerulea*
Year Made State Flower: 1899

The dazzling Rocky Mountain columbine is a perfect match for the blue skies and snowy peaks of Colorado's high country.

Rocky Mountain columbine grows as low as 1,000 feet (305 meters) above sea level, but the flowers are bluest in the mountains up to 11,000 feet (3,353 meters).

The columbine stands up to 24 inches (61 centimeters) tall. The flower itself may be 3 inches (8 centimeters) across.

Rocky Mountain columbine blooms from mid-June into mid-August. The high altitude plants bloom last.

CONNECTICUT
MOUNTAIN LAUREL

Scientific Name: *Kalmia latifolia*
Year Made State Flower: 1907

After the rush of spring wildflowers fades on the floors of Connecticut's woodlands, the mountain laurel shrubs steal the spotlight with their clusters of pinkish-white blossoms. Mountain laurel lights up forests throughout much of the East in June. Mountain laurel is also the state flower of Pennsylvania (p. 36).

The large evergreen mountain laurel shrubs may stand 15 feet (about 5 meters) tall.

DELAWARE
PEACH BLOSSOM

Scientific Name:
Prunus persica
Year Made State Flower:
1985

Delaware is a major producer of peaches. Early each spring its peach groves are colored by the pink blossoms of the peach trees.

Peach blossoms are small with five petals. Each blossom looks like a tiny wild rose.

Peach trees stand 15 to 25 feet (5 - 8 meters) tall. The first peach trees were probably brought to North America by the Spanish explorers in the 1500's.

FLORIDA
ORANGE BLOSSOM

Scientific Name:
Citrus sinensis
Year Made State Flower:
1909

(Florida continued)

Spanish settlers brought the first orange trees to Florida in the 1500's. Nearly 400 years later, the state of Florida adopted the orange blossom as its state flower. Little did the Spanish know that their plantings would lead to a multibillion dollar industry.

Florida is the leading producer of oranges in the United States. Each spring its orange trees produce millions of small, white blossoms that fill the air with a sweet scent.

GEORGIA
CHEROKEE ROSE

Scientific Name:
Rosa sinica
Year Made State Flower:
1916

The roots of Georgia's state flower, the Cherokee rose, can be followed back to China. But long before Georgia became a state, the Native American Cherokees had gotten the plant and spread it throughout the region.

Like other wild roses, the Cherokee rose produces a tasty fruit called a hip. The fruit was a popular food with Native Americans.

The Cherokee rose is a prickly, climbing shrub. It blooms in spring and sometimes again in autumn.

HAWAII
YELLOW HIBISCUS

Scientific Name: *Hibiscus brackenridgei*
Year Made State Flower: 1988

The yellow hibiscus, Hawaii's state flower, is one of hundreds of varieties of hibiscus developed by plant lovers in Hawaii. This particular hibiscus is raised as a shrub and planted in gardens, yards, and public places.

The yellow hibiscus blossom looks like a hand-sized pinwheel. It's a big, strikingly attractive flower that blooms on a long, narrow stem.

Hibiscus are popular garden flowers in many of the mainland states where frost is rare or unknown.

IDAHO
SYRINGA

Scientific Name: *Philadelphus lewisii*
Year Made State Flower: 1931

The syringa is a Western shrub first noticed and recorded by explorer Meriwhether Lewis during the famous Lewis and Clark expedition of 1803-06.

The syringa has clusters of four-petalled, white flowers. Each flower blossom is from 1 to 2 inches (3 - 5 centimeters) across and produces a sweet fragrance.

Blooms of syringa brighten the sides of hills and streams in Idaho. The shrub grows on mountain slopes as high as 7,000 feet (2,134 meters).

Native Americans of the West used syringa stems for arrow shafts.

ILLINOIS
NATIVE VIOLET (SISTER VIOLET)

Scientific Name:
  Viola sororia
Year Made State Flower:
  1908

Illinois' state flower is a common spring wildflower in the state's rich, moist forests. It is sometimes called the native violet, sister violet, or blue violet. Actually, many species of wild blue violets grow in Illinois.

Blue violets bloom on stems that rarely stretch more than 8 inches (20.5 centimeters). Their color has made them springtime favorites.
(See New Jersey, p. 30; Rhode Island, p. 37; and Wisconsin, p. 46.)

INDIANA
PEONY

Scientific Name:
  Paeonia group
Year Made State Flower:
  1957

(Indiana continued)

Peonies are big, brightly colored garden flowers. The plants grow to 4 feet (over a meter) tall and more in trees and bush peonies.

Many varieties of peonies are planted in Indiana and elsewhere. Some have "double blossoms," or several layers of petals.

The most familiar peonies are red, or crimson. They begin to bloom at the end of May.

IOWA
WILD ROSE

Scientific Name:
Rosa group
Year Made State Flower:
1897

When Iowans chose the wild rose as their state flower, they did not select one particular kind. That is just as well. Native wild roses look quite similar to each other, and all of them are beautiful pink or white flowers.

Wild roses have five petals around a yellow center. They grow in thickets. Their blossoms are lighter in color and more delicate than those of garden roses.

(See New York, p. 32; and North Dakota, p. 33.)

KANSAS
NATIVE SUNFLOWER

Scientific Name: *Helianthus annuus*
Year Made State Flower: 1903

Sunflowers are tall, showy flowers that love the open spaces and grasslands of Kansas. Kansas pioneers loved the bright yellow blossoms that nodded above the endless waves of prairie grasses.

Sunflowers begin blooming in July. Some are still in bloom as the prairie grass begins to yellow in September.

Wild sunflowers can stand 10 feet (3 meters) tall. Sunflower farmers grow their domestic sunflowers even bigger. Sunflowers are raised for their seeds and oil.

KENTUCKY
GOLDENROD OR TALL GOLDENROD

Scientific Name: *Solidago altissima*
Year Made State Flower: 1926

The goldenrods are a group of late-blooming wildflowers that brighten roadsides and clearings with splashes of golden yellow. Kentucky's state flower, the tall goldenrod, is one of several goldenrod species found in Kentucky. The species are often hard to tell apart.

Like its cousins, the tall goldenrod has clusters of small yellow flowers that grow on arching branches. Well named, the tall goldenrod can reach heights of 7 feet (2 meters). (See Nebraska, p. 27.)

LOUISIANA
SOUTHERN MAGNOLIA

Scientific Name: *Magnolia grandiflora*
Year Made State Flower: 1900

The wide white flowers of magnolia trees are familiar symbols of the Deep South. They are the state flower of Louisiana and Mississippi.

Magnolia trees themselves are no less striking than the blossoms. Magnolias have thick, waxy leaves that help give these trees a stately appearance.

Magnolia trees can stand up to 125 feet (38 meters) tall. (See Mississippi, p. 25.)

MAINE
WHITE PINE CONE AND TASSEL

Scientific Name: *Pinus strobus*
Year Made State Flower: 1925

The white pine tree is highly regarded in Maine, where logging is an important industry. The white pine is the state tree, and it appears on the state seal. Its cone and springtime tassel are Maine's state "flower," chosen first in 1894 and adopted by the Maine legislature in 1925.

The white pine is a tall, straight tree with broad layers of limbs. Its white wood is highly prized for lumber.

MARYLAND
BLACK-EYED SUSAN

Scientific Name:
Rudbeckia hirta
Year Made State Flower:
1918

Bright yellow with a chocolate center, the flowers of black-eyed Susans lend summertime color to the fields and open woods of Maryland.

The black-eyed Susan looks much like a yellow daisy, to which it is related. It is also related to sunflowers with its circle of long, narrow petals.

The flowers of the plant are about 3 inches (7 - 8 centimeters) across. The black-eyed Susan stands from 1 to 3 feet (30 - 90 centimeters) tall.

MASSACHUSETTS
MAYFLOWER (TRAILING ARBUTUS)

Scientific Name:
Epigaea repens
Year Made State Flower:
1918

(Massachusetts continued)

Massachusetts' state flower is a low-to-the-ground, creeping plant with small white or pink flowers and small, leathery evergreen leaves. The plant is often called mayflower in New England. Elsewhere in the East it is better known by the name trailing arbutus.

The mayflower blooms as early as March. In the mountains it blooms as late as May.

Mayflower blossoms "hide" among the leaves. By rustling through dry winter leaves under mayflower stems, one can uncover the tiny five-petaled flowers.

MICHIGAN

APPLE BLOSSOM

Scientific Name:
Malus domestica

Year Made State Flower:
1897

Next to Washington state, Michigan is the leading apple producer in the United States. The fall apple crop is important to the state's economy. But Michiganders love the apple tree's blossoms as well as its fruit.

Michigan orchards look snow-decked each May when the apple orchards bloom.

(See Arkansas, p. 8.)

MINNESOTA
SHOWY LADY'S-SLIPPER
(PINK AND WHITE LADY'S-SLIPPER)

Scientific Name: *Cypripedium reginae*
Year Made State Flower: 1902

Minnesota's state flower, the showy lady's-slipper, is truly one of the most beautiful of North American wildflowers.

The lady's-slipper is a wild orchid. Larger greenhouse orchids are used in corsages.

The showy lady's-slipper is the largest of the species of North American lady's-slippers. This plant grows in moist woods and bogs. The plant may be up to 3 feet (91 centimeters) tall. In Minnesota, most of the showy lady's-slippers bloom in June.

MISSISSIPPI
SOUTHERN MAGNOLIA

Scientific Name: *Magnolia grandiflora*
Year Made State Flower: 1952

Old Southern towns often have their streets lined with magnolia trees. Magnolia trees grace Southern lawns and woodlands, too, where they grow wild among other native trees. Magnolias are as much a part of the South as grits and Spanish moss.

Mississippi honored the magnolia as both its state flower and its state tree.

(See Louisiana, p. 20.)

MISSOURI
HAWTHORN

Scientific Name:
  Crataegus group
Year Made State Flower:
  1923

Like several other states, Missouri chose the striking blossom of a tree as its state flower.

Missouri's choice, the hawthorn, is sometimes described as a shrub rather than a tree.

Several species of hawthorns grow in Missouri and elsewhere in North America. They are hard to tell apart, but all of them share five-petaled flowers that look like little apple blossoms.

Hawthorns grow best in open sunny areas. Many are planted as yard trees.

MONTANA
BITTERROOT

Scientific Name:
  Lewisia rediviva
Year Made State Flower:
  1895

(Montana continued)

The bitterroot is especially common in Montana's western mountains.

The roots of the plant were eaten by Native Americans. Today the plant is better known for its showy pink blossoms.

Bitterroot blooms from late April in the lowlands into early July in the mountains. Flowers of 1 to 2 inches (3 - 5 centimeters) across bloom on short stems.

Bitterroot grows up to 8,000 feet (2,438 meters).

NEBRASKA

GOLDENROD OR LATE GOLDENROD

Scientific Name:
Solidago gigantea
Year Made State Flower:
1895

In Nebraska, a state of broad fields and prairies, the goldenrod adds late summer banners of yellow-gold. The flower heads of late goldenrod are just one-quarter inch (less than 1 centimeter) wide. Each plant bears hundreds of flowers to brighten the landscape wherever it grows.

Nebraska's goldenrod is closely related to the tall goldenrod, Kentucky's (p. 19) state flower. Several kinds of goldenrod grow in Nebraska.

NEVADA
SAGEBRUSH OR BIG SAGEBRUSH

Scientific Name: *Artemisia tridentata*
Year Made State Flower: 1917

Nevada's state flower, the big sagebrush, is a common bushy plant of plains and mountain valleys. Several kinds of sagebrush grow in Nevada and the American West. This species has gray-green leaves and tiny silver-green flowers. The bush may stand 10 feet (3 meters) tall.

The flowers of big sagebrush bloom in August and September, signaling the end of summer on the plains.

Sagebrush has a pleasant tangy smell when it is wet. The plant can be used for fuel and even for tea.

NEW HAMPSHIRE
PURPLE LILAC

Scientific Name: *Syringa vulgaris*
Year Made State Flower: 1919

Lilac blossoms are sure signs of May in New Hampshire. They may be white, deep purple, or purple-blue.

Lilac blossoms bloom on shrubs. The plant may be 20 feet (6 meters) tall.

Lilacs are ornamental plants because they are used to make gardens, yards, and public places more attractive. Lilacs are common in many northern states.

NEW JERSEY
NATIVE VIOLET (SISTER VIOLET)

Scientific Name: *Viola sororia*
Year Made State Flower: 1913

New Jersey is one of four states to have adopted a native blue violet as its state flower. New Jersey's violet is the same species as Illinois' (p. 16).

The native, or sister, violet blooms in spring. It lives in moist meadows and moist, open woodlands.
(See Rhode Island, p. 37; and Wisconsin, p. 46.)

NEW MEXICO
YUCCA OR SOAP WEED

Scientific Name: *Yucca elata*
Year Made State Flower: 1927

The yucca plant is common in the Southwest. It belongs to the lily family but, looks nothing like a lily. New Mexico's state flower has the typical spiny leaves of yuccas.

Roots of the yucca were once used to make soap, so it is sometimes called soap weed. Native Americans in New Mexico and elsewhere wove the dried yucca leaves into mats and roasted parts of the stem for food.

Clusters of yucca flowers blossom on a tall stalk above the leaves, or "needles." The creamy blooms appear in June and July.

NEW YORK
WILD ROSE

Scientific Name:
Rosa group
Year Made State Flower:
1955

Many species of wild roses grow in New York state. Their flowers may be red, pink, or white. All of them, however, share equally the honor of state flower. When New York chose the wild rose for its state flower, it wisely did not single out one species.

The flowers of wild rose bushes are 2 to 3 inches (5 - 8 centimeters) across. They begin to bloom in late spring. The red fruits of wild roses, called hips, are used for jellies. (See Iowa, p. 17; and North Dakota, p. 33.)

NORTH CAROLINA
FLOWERING DOGWOOD

Scientific Name:
Cornus florida
Year Made State Flower:
1941

The white blossoms of flowering dogwood are heralds of spring in the woodlands of North Carolina. The peak of the bloom is usually in late April.

The flowering dogwood is a small, slender tree of the forest floor. It is a beloved tree throughout much of the East and lower Midwest. Dogwood is also the state flower of Virginia (p. 43).

NORTH DAKOTA
WILD PRAIRIE ROSE

Scientific Name:
  Rosa blanda and
  others
Year Made State Flower:
  1907

North Dakota is a state of wide green prairies. In early summer wild roses dot the grasslands with pink blossoms.

Several kinds of wild roses grow in North Dakota. They are all commonly known as wild or prairie roses, although one species is also called the smooth rose. It lacks the thorns of most roses, wild and domestic.

(See Iowa, p. 17; and New York, p. 32.)

OHIO
SCARLET CARNATION

Scientific Name: *Dianthus caryophyllus*
Year Made State Flower: 1904

Ohio's state flower, the scarlet carnation, honors one of the state's favorite sons, William McKinley.

Mr. McKinley, born in Niles, Ohio, became the 25th president of the United States. He was killed by an assassin in 1901.

President McKinley loved red carnations and he often wore one on his coat.

Carnations are still extremely popular flowers. Greenhouses grow millions of carnations in the United States each year.

OKLAHOMA
MISTLETOE

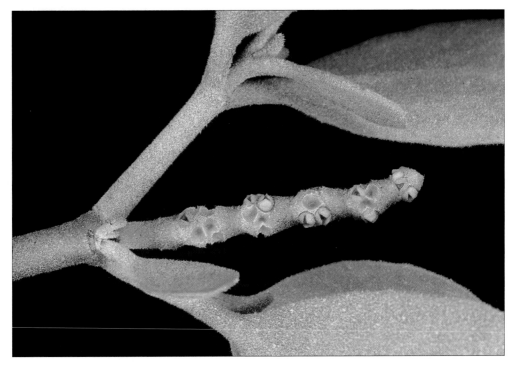

Scientific Name: *Phoradendron serotinum*
Year Made State Flower: 1893

Mistletoe is a small, bushy plant that grows in tangles on the branches of trees. In Oklahoma, it almost always chooses an elm tree as its host.

Mistletoe blooms in February or March. Its yellow flowers are the size of pinheads. Tall tales from Europe about its power—rather than its flowers—likely led Oklahomans to adopt mistletoe.

Now the plant is best known for its small, white berries and its use as an evergreen decoration at Christmas. Tradition throughout the U.S. holds that anyone who stands under mistletoe risks being kissed.

OREGON
OREGON GRAPE

Scientific Name:
Berberis aquifolium
Year Made State Flower:
1899

The Oregon grape is not a true grape. It's a low-lying shrub that produces berries. Sometimes, like grapes, the berries are used for jam.

The Oregon grape shrub produces bright yellow flowers, each with six petals. Long after the flowers disappear, the Oregon grape adds more color to the Oregon landscape: bright red leaves each autumn.

PENNSYLVANIA
MOUNTAIN LAUREL

Scientific Name:
Kalmia latifolia
Year Made State Flower:
1933

(Pennsylvania continued)

Pennsylvania's green mountains are speckled each June with the buds and blossoms of mountain laurel. Mountain laurel is related to the rhododendrons, which also bloom in early summer.

Although a native wild shrub, mountain laurel is often transplanted to yards and public places because of its beauty. (See Connecticut, p. 11)

Rhode Island
Early Blue Violet

Scientific Name:
Viola palmata
Year Made State Flower:
1968

The early blue violet blooms in April and May. It is a familiar spring wildflower in much of the eastern United States.

Four states have adopted blue violets as their state flowers. Rhode Island, however, is the only state to have chosen this particular species of blue violet.

(See Illinois, p. 16; New Jersey, p. 30; and Wisconsin, p. 46.)

SOUTH CAROLINA
YELLOW JESSAMINE

Scientific Name:
Gelsemium sempervirens
Year Made State Flower:
1924

The sweet scent and bright flowers of the yellow jessamine are among the first signs of spring in South Carolina.

The vines of the yellow jessamine produce trumpet-shaped blossoms. The vine itself trails around trees, fences, and thickets.

SOUTH DAKOTA
PASQUEFLOWER

Scientific Name:
Anemone patens
Year Made State Flower:
1903

(South Dakota continued)

The cheery white blossoms of pasqueflowers are among the first blooms of spring in South Dakota. They are among the most beautiful of spring wildflowers.

Pasqueflowers bloom on the old prairies in March and April. Their blossoms huddle close to the ground, nearly hidden in the still-brown tangles of the prairie grass.

Pasqueflower blossoms are up to 2-1/2 inches (about 6 centimeters) wide. The stems are often just 6 to 8 inches (15 - 20 centimeters) long.

TENNESSEE
IRIS (BLUEFLAG)

Scientific Name:
Iridaceae family
Year Made State Flower:
1933

Several species of wild iris grow in the moist woodlands and swampy meadows of Tennessee. Several hundred kinds of garden iris also bloom in the state. Both wild and garden-grown varieties are state flowers.

Wild irises or blueflags, are usually a shade of purple or blue. Garden varieties may be blue, purple, yellow, white, wine-red, or some combination of these colors.

Iris flowers may be as little as 1 inch (less than 3 centimeters) across or as big as 12 inches (31 centimeters) across. Irises may be 6 inches (about 15 centimeters) or 6 feet (almost 2 meters) tall.

TEXAS
BLUEBONNET (LUPINE)

Scientific Name: *Lupinus* group
Year Made State Flower: 1901

Bluebonnets brighten the Texas fields and plains with great carpets of lavender and blue blossoms each spring.

Texas is home to several species of wild bluebonnets. In 1971 the state expanded from one to five its official list of bluebonnets that are honored as state flowers. The five that share the honor are *Lupinus subcarnusus, L. texensis, L. harvardii, L. concinnus,* and *L. plattensis.* Certainly there are some differences among the plants, but to Texans, the chosen five and the unchosen, too, are all blue beauties.

Bluebonnet flowers bloom in clusters on stalks.

UTAH
SEGO LILY OR MARIPOSA LILY

Scientific Name: *Calochortus nuttallii*
Year Made State Flower: 1911

The sego lily, Utah's state flower, has an attractive tuliplike blossom growing on a long, wire-thin stem.

The sego lily's bulb-shaped root is sweet and full of vitamins. It was a popular food with Native Americans in the region and Utah pioneers.

The sego lily blooms in June and early July on plains and hillsides.

VERMONT
RED CLOVER

Scientific Name: *Trifolium pratense*
Year Made State Flower: 1894

The red clover is a familiar plant of meadows and roadsides. The round-headed, candlelike blooms of red clover first show up in May. Red clover continues blooming into September.

Red clover is not native to North America, although it is widespread in North America. The plant was imported from Europe. Early American settlers used dried clover heads for tea.

Red clover is widely planted for farm animals' food and to enrich soil.

VIRGINIA
FLOWERING DOGWOOD

Scientific Name: *Cornus florida*
Year Made State Flower: 1918

In springtime, flowering dogwood brightens the rolling Virginia countryside with its white blossoms. In autumn the trees' red berries and red leaves add vivid color to the woodlands.

The wood of this tree was once used for daggers. The name dogwood probably came from "dagwood," a short form of "dagger-wood." (See North Carolina, p. 32.)

WASHINGTON
COAST RHODODENDRON

Scientific Name: *Rhododendron macrophyllum*
Year Made State Flower: 1949

Washington's state flower, the coast rhododendron, is an evergreen shrub that grows in the state's moist coastal forests. Coast rhododendron has dark green, waxy leaves and large pink or rose-colored blossoms.

The shrubs stand 4 to 12 feet (about 1 to 4 meters) tall. They can be found along America's Pacific coast from Washington south into the groves of giant redwood trees in Northern California.

On the other side of the continent, West Virginia (p. 46) honors another species of rhododendron as its state flower.

WASHINGTON, D.C.
AMERICAN BEAUTY ROSE

Scientific Name: *Rosa* family
Year Made State Flower: 1925

The big, colorful roses of gardens and greenhouses are among America's favorite flowers. The District of Columbia chose one of them, the dark pink American Beauty rose, as its official flower.

The American Beauty was imported to the United States from France in 1882 as the Madam Ferdinand Jamin rose. Rose growers had a difficult time selling it until changing its name, in 1885, to the American Beauty. The new name made the rose a great success for many years.

Today the American Beauty is fairly hard to find, mainly because it is a difficult rose to grow outdoors.

WEST VIRGINIA

ROSEBAY RHODODENDRON (BIG LAUREL)

Scientific Name:
Rhododendron maximum

Year Made State Flower:
1903

Rhododendrons love the rugged mountains of the Southeast. These evergreen shrubs make dense, tangled thickets in ravines, along brooks, and on mountain slopes. Their big light pink and white blossoms appear in June and July.

The rosebay rhododendron grows throughout much of West Virginia's hill country and the southern Appalachian Mountains. Rosebay thickets can reach heights of 5,000 feet (1,524 meters).

WISCONSIN

WOOD VIOLET OR COMMON BLUE VIOLET

Scientific Name:
Viola papilionacea

Year Made State Flower:
1908

(Wisconsin continued)

Wisconsin's state flower, the wood violet, is a widespread wildflower throughout the eastern United States and westward to Minnesota and Oklahoma. It usually blossoms in Wisconsin in May and June.

The wood violet may be blue, but it also may be pure white or white with purple veins.

Violets are the wild relatives of a familiar garden flower, the pansy. Violets have much smaller blossoms than pansies, though.

WYOMING

INDIAN PAINTBRUSH (PAINTED-CUP)

Scientific Name:
   Castilleja linariaefolia
Year Made State Flower:
   1917

The paintbrushes are a colorful group of wildflowers that live mostly in the American West. More than two dozen kinds of paintbrush live in the Rocky Mountains alone, including yellow and purple-pink species.

Wyoming's state flower is one of the red species of paintbrush. The red flowers are actually broad red leaves at the plant's tip.

Paintbrush grows on slender stalks 1 to 3 feet (31 - 92 centimeters) tall. The plant lives on the plains and in mountains up to 9,000 feet (2,473 meters) high.

INDEX